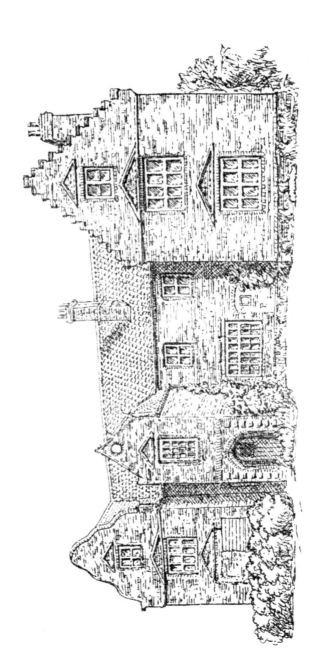

Hindolveston Manor-house

See also p. 34

THREE GENERATIONS

R. W. Ketton-Cremer

Additional material on the Astley family and Melton Constable

by

David Yaxley

The Larks Press

First 1,000 copies printed and published by
The Larks Press
Ordnance Farm House, Guist Bottom, Dereham,
Norfolk NR20 5PF
November 1992

ISBN 0 948400 18 8

Preface

'Three Generations' was written by R.W.Ketton-Cremer in 1958 and printed privately for him in December of that year for distribution to his friends as a 'sort of Christmas card'. In his own preface to that edition he expresses his gratitude to the late Dowager Lady Hastings for allowing him to make use of the letters quoted in this study. He also writes, 'I have in general retained their original spelling; but all contracted words have been lengthened, and other minor adjustments made. I have also added some punctuation at certain points.'

This present edition is published with the permission of the Royal Literary Fund which holds the copyright.

CONTENTS

———◆———

An Introduction to the Astley Family

Melton Constable gets the first part of its name from the Old English *mael-tun*, 'town with a mark or cross', or *mylentun*, 'town with a mill', and the second part from its association since at least 1197 with the hereditary constable of the bishop of Norwich. The family of de Mealton was sometimes called 'le Constable' or 'de Constable' in the 12th and 13th centuries, and its head acted as the arm of the bishop in both military and civil matters. The Astley family, which was seated in Warwickshire since the 12th century, acquired Melton Constable by the marriage of Sir Thomas Astley of Hillmorton to Editha, sister and co-heir of Sir Robert Constable, the last male representative of the de Constables. Sir Thomas died fighting for Simon de Montfort at the Battle of Evesham in 1265, and the Melton Constable estate descended by his second son Ralph through several generations to Thomas Astley, who died in 1501. The subsequent generations of Astleys will be found in the following pedigree.

In the 16th century marriage brought connexions with several families that were rich and important, both locally and nationally. Anne Wood, second wife of Thomas Astley (d. 1543), was sister-in-law to Sir James Boleyn of Blickling, uncle to Queen Anne Boleyn and brother to Lady Shelton, who was governess to Princess Mary Tudor, the daughter of Henry VIII and Katherine of Aragon. John Astley (d.1595) and his first wife Catherine Champernown held positions in the household of the young Princess Elizabeth. They were staunch protestants, and went abroad during the reign of the Roman Catholic Mary Tudor. but on Elizabeth's accession in 1558 John was appointed Master of the Jewel

House and treasurer of the Queen's jewels and plate; other offices and grants of land, including estates in Kent and the old palace of Maidstone, followed. He was also the author of a book on the Art of Riding (1584). Isaac Astley (*c.*1540–98) married Mary Waldegrave, whose father was second cousin to Sir Edward Waldegrave, Master of the Great Wardrobe and Chancellor of the Duchy of Lancaster under Mary Tudor. The marriage may have been arranged by William Butts of Thornage, just four miles from Melton; Butts was one of the three sons of Sir William Butts (physician to Henry VIII and his queens, Princess Mary, Wolsey, the Duke of Norfolk &c.), who married three sisters of the Bures family, cousins to Mary Waldegrave. The Waldegrave family had an estate at Stanninghall, and Charles Waldegrave married Jeromina Jerningham of Costessey Hall. Isaac and Mary had at least 15 children; five died in infancy, but nine, not including the eldest son Thomas, are mentioned in Isaac's will of 1597. (1) The best known of the sons was Sir Jacob Astley (1579-1653), one of the royal commanders in the Civil War, and the highlights of his career as a professional soldier are set out by Mr Ketton-Cremer in the following pages. The sons of his brother Thomas (1567-1617) were important in local affairs. The eldest, Francis, died in 1638 in the middle of his term as Sheriff of Norfolk, and his brothers, Isaac and Edward, were very active in Norfolk during the Civil War and Interregnum. Their activities, and those of Sir Jacob, form the substance of Mr Ketton-Cremer's book.

———◆———

1. The list in the pedigree is based on the Melton Constable register. The late Lord Hastings, in his '*Astley of Melton Constable 1236-1936*' gives Isaac 9 sons and 8 daughters; the 3rd son, he says, was Edward, who went to Palestine with

Henry Bacon; Bacon died at Jerusalem, and Edward in the Low Countries. There is no mention of an Edward in the registers, nor is he mentioned in Isaac's will of 1597 (ex. inf. A. Hassell Smith). The only Henry Bacon of the right period was the third son of Sir Nicholas Bacon, son of Sir Nicholas the Lord Keeper and premier baronet; Henry was born in 1570, but I can find no record of his death in Jerusalem. Similarly, I have been unable to find any confirmation of Lord Hastings' assertion that Waldegrave Astley became a colonel in the royalist forces in the Civil War. The history of Isaac's daughters is even more shadowy. Lord Hastings' claim that Isaac gave away six manors as dower with his daughters seems to run contrary to the evidence; of the manors he names (according to Blomefield) Langham Snitterley, Glandford, and possibly Wiveton were sold by Isaac to the Calthorpe family around 1588-9, none of whom are recorded as marrying Isaac's daughters, even if any of them had been old enough to marry before he died; Nowers manor, Hindringham, was sold to Sir Roger Townshend in 1538-9 by Thomas and John Astley, and Brinningham never seems to have left Astley hands

Pedigree since 1500

Thomas Astley, d. 1501, m. 1. Margery, dau. of William Lumnor of Mannington and 2. Elizabeth, dau. of William Clipesby of Oby Esq. He was succeeded by his eldest son by his 1st wife

Thomas Astley, d. 1543, m. 1. Anne Boughton, by whom he had John Astley d. *c.*1558 *(see below)*.
By his 2nd wife Anne, dau. of John Woode of East Barsham, who d. 1512, he had

John Astley, d. 1595, courtier and writer, who m. 1. Catherine, dau. of Sir Philip Champernown of Devon, by whom he had no issue; and 2. Margaret, dau. of Thomas, Lord Grey, by whom he had
Sir John Astley, d. without issue 1639, and three daughters.

John Astley, d. *c.*1558, succeeded his father 1543; m. Frances, dau. of John Chene or Cheyney of Sittingbourne, Kent, by whom he had

Isaac Astley, *c.* **1540 - 98,** m. Mary, 3rd dau. of Edward Waldegrave of Lawford, Essex, by whom he had
1. Thomas, 1567-1617
2. John, b. 1568, perhaps living 1597
3. Francis, 1571-3
4. Anne, b. 1572, d. before 1577
5. Marie, b. 1574, d. before 1585
6. Ann, b. 1577
7. Francis, 1577-8
8. Jacob, 1579-1653
9. Francis, b. 1581, living 1597
10. Isaac, b. 1583, living 1597)
11. Abraham, b. 1583, living 1597) twins
12. Marie, b. 1585, living 1597
13. Walgrave, b. 1587, living 1597

14. Richard, b. 1592 *(see below)*
15. Jane, b. 1594, living 1597
16. ?Edward, perhaps d. 1599 (see note 1 to introduction)

Isaac d. 1598 and was succeeded by his eldest son,

Thomas Astley, 1567-1617, m. 18 June 1593 Frances (b. 1579), dau. of Edward Deane of Tilney, by her he had

1. Sir Francis, 1595-1638, m. Elizabeth dau. of Sir John Altham; d. without issue
2. Marie, 1596-8
3. Dorothie, b. 1598, living 1643
4. Sir Isaac 1600-59, baronet 1641; m. 1. Rachel, dau. of Augustine Messenger of Hackford. She d. 1639. He m. 2. Bridget, dau. of John Coke of Holkham; she d. 1700. No issue by either marriage
5. Marie, b. 1602
6. Edward, b. 1604 or 1605, d. 1654. *(see below)*
7. Thomas, d. 1516

Sir Jacob Astley, 1579-1653, 8th child and 2nd surviving son of Isaac Astley, created Baron Astley of Reading 1644; m. Agnes Imple or Impel of Bloumerckem, Netherlands, and by her had

1. Isaac, 2nd Baron Astley, d. 1662; m. Anne, dau. of Sir Francis Stydolfe of Norberry, Surrey, and had by her Jacob 1652-88, 3rd and last Baron Astley, m. Frances, dau. of Sir Richard Stydolfe, and d. without issue
2. Thomas, died in Holland
3. Sir Bernard, d. unmarried 1645
4. Elizabeth *c.* 1619-84, m. Edward Astley *(see below)*

Richard Astley, b. 1592, 14th child and 3rd surviving son of Isaac; m. Jane — d. 1660

M.A., ordained by Bishop of Norwich 1617, pres. to rectories of Melton Constable and Burgh Parva 1617; licensed to preach by Bp. of Norwich 1620. Resigned Melton Constable 1642, Burgh Parva 1652.

Edward Astley, 1604 or 1605-1654. Knighted 1641; m. Elizabeth *c.* 1619-84, dau. of Sir Jacob Astley, by whom he had

1. Sir Jacob Astley 1640-1729 *(see below)*
2. Frances 1642-5
3. Thomas d. 1645
4. John d. 1646
5. Agnita d. 1648

Sir Jacob Astley, 1640-1729, baronet 1660; m. Blanche *c.* 1642-97, eldest dau. of Sir Philip Wodehouse of Kimberley, by whom he had

1. Jacob *c.* 1663-81
2. Sir Philip 1667-1739 *(see below)*
3. Edward d. 1673
4. Blanche b. 1672
5. Elizabeth b. 1676
6. John

Sir Philip Astley, 1667-1739, 2nd baronet m. Elizabeth, dau. of Thomas Bransby of Caistor, Norfolk, by whom, (who d. 1738), he had

1. Sir Jacob 1692-1760 *(see below)*
2. Elizabeth, b.1693, m. Caleb Elwin of Thurning (d.1776)
3. Philip b. 1694
4. Blanch b. 1695
5. Edward b. 1699
6. Thomas b. 1700.
7. Jemima b. 1703 m. Christopher Metcalf of Horstead

Sir Jacob Astley 1692-1760, 3rd baronet; m. 1. Lucy, youngest dau. of Sir Nicholas Le Strange of Hunstanton & coheir of her brother Sir Henry Le Strange, and by her (who d. 1739) he had

1. Sir Edward 1729-1802. *(see below)*
2. John d. 1803, rector of Thornage, m. Catherine dau. of

Philip Bell of Wallington

3. Blanch m. Edward Pratt of Ryston

Sir Jacob m.2. Judith, dau. of Isaac Watlington and widow of Gresham Page; she d. without issue 1743. He m. 3. (1744) Sarah, dau. of Christopher Bedingfield; she d. 1764 without issue.

Sir Edward Astley, 1729-1802, 4th baronet; m. 1. Rhoda, eldest dau. of Francis Blake Delaval of Seaton Delaval, Northumberland. She d. 1757 having had

1. Sir Jacob Henry, 5th baronet 1756-1817 *(see below)*
2. Francis d. 1778 in the fight of the *Arethusa* against the the French frigate *La Belle Poule.*

Sir Edward m. 2. Anne, youngest dau. of Christopher Milles of North Elmham and Nackington, Kent; she d.1793 having had three sons. Sir Edward m. 3. Elizabeth Bullen who d. 1810 without issue.

Sir Jacob Henry Astley, 1756-1817, 5th baronet m, Sarah, dau. of Samuel Browne of King's Lynn. She d. 1855 having had

1. Sir Jacob 1797-1859, 6th baronet *(see below)*
2. Edward 1799-1846
3. Francis L'Estrange 1810-66 m. Charlotte Micklethwaite
4. Rhoda d. 1808
5. Anne d. 1833 m. Thomas Macqueen
6. Editha d. 1871, m. Warden Sergison
7. Blanch d. 1870
8. Hester d. 1867 m. Revd Augustus Dashwood
9. Agnes d. 1872, m. Revd John Henry Sparke

Sir Jacob Astley, 1797-1859, 6th baronet and 16th baron Hastings (1841), m. Georgiana Caroline; 2nd dau. of Sir Henry Watkin Dashwood, and had

1. Jacob Henry Delaval 1822-71, 17th baron Hastings, m. Frances Cosham; d. without issue and was succeeded by his brother

2. Delaval Loftus 1825-72, M.A., vicar of East Barsham, 18th Baron Hastings. He m. Frances Diana Manners-Sutton 2nd dau. of Viscount Canterbury, and by her had

1. Bernard Edward Delaval Astley 1855-75, 19th baron Hastings, d. without issue
2. George Manners Astley 1857-1904, 20th baron Hastings *(see below)*
3. Henry Jacob 1867-1909 m. Sybil Fountaine, d. without issue
4. Agneta Frances m. Roland Le Strange

George Manners Astley, 1857-1904, 20th baron Hastings, m. Elizabeth Harbord, 3rd dau. of Charles Harbord, 5th Lord Suffield, and had

1. Albert Edward Delaval, 1882-1956, 21st baron Hastings *(see below)*
2. Jacob John 1884-1917
3. Charles Merton b. 1885
4. Alexandra Rhoda b.1886
5. Bridget 1889-1906
6. Hester Winifred b. 1899

Albert Edward Delaval Astley, 1812-1956, 21st baron Hastings m. Marguerite Helen Nevill, dau. of Marquess of Abergavenny, by whom he had

Edward Delaval Henry Astley, b. 1912, 22nd baron Hastings, m. Catherine Rosaline Radcliffe, younger dau. of Capt. Harold Hinton, and has

1. Delaval Thomas Harold b. 1960
2. Harriet Marguerite, b. 1958
3. Justin, b. 1968

ERRATA
p. iv Lines 20 & 27 — insert *(see below)*

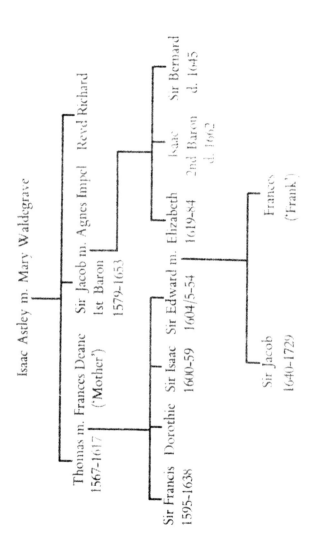

A much-simplified family tree

Isaac Astley m. Mary Waldegrave

Thomas m. Frances Deane   Sir Jacob m. Agnes Impel   Revd Richard
1567-1617   ('Mother')   1st Baron
                                 1579-1653

Sir Francis Dorothie Sir Isaac Sir Edward m. Elizabeth   Isaac   Sir Bernard
1595-1638   1600-59   1604/5-54   1619-84   2nd Baron   d. 1645
                                                             d. 1662

                    Sir Jacob   Frances
                    1640-1729   ('Frank')

THREE GENERATIONS

I

Throughout the Civil War, the political and religious differences which had broken the nation asunder were reflected in the private life of many English families. Sometimes the disagreement had a regional basis. An East Anglian family, for example, would be united in support of the Parliament, while their cousins in the West Country were fervent partisans of the King. But there were also many instances of complete division between close relations who lived in the same immediate neighbourhood, between father and son, brother and brother. Sometimes the sympathies of a woman would be cruelly torn between the claims of her husband and her own kindred.

The story of the Astley family during the war discloses just such a conflict of loyalties. It was less tragic than many situations of the kind, since little personal bitterness appears to have been involved. Nevertheless during four long years it was the fate of Elizabeth Lady Astley that her husband (who was also her cousin) should be actively engaged in the service of the Parliament, while her father was one of the King's most trusted generals, and her brother died for the royal cause. Since she was devoted to them all, her position at times must indeed have been a sad one. But the bonds of love and consanguinity alike held firm. The family was reunited directly the conflict came to an end, and reunited especially in affection for the small boy who represents the third generation in the ensuing pages.

The eminent royalist commander who was to become Sir Jacob Astley, and subsequently Lord Astley of Reading, was born in 1579, one of the younger sons of a Norfolk gentleman, Isaac Astley of Melton Constable. Like many English youths of martial temperament he sought his fortune overseas, first in the armies of the States-General of the Netherlands, and later in the service of the Elector Palatine. For almost forty years his courage and ability as a soldier carried him all over Europe. At one time he served with King Christian IV of Denmark, at another with Gustavus Adolphus of Sweden. In the intervals of this career of battles, sieges, skirmishes and marches he was domiciled in the Netherlands, where he married a lady named Agnes Impel. They had two sons, Isaac and Bernard, and a daughter Elizabeth.

He was regarded with high favour by the young Elector Palatine and his wife, Charles I's sister Elizabeth, the 'Winter Queen' of Bohemia. As a seasoned professional soldier he appears to have supervised the martial exercises of her son Prince Rupert, and is described as his governor or tutor. A letter written to him in 1627 from The Hague by the Queen of Bohemia has survived. She addresses him as 'Honest little Jacob,' and indulges in some rather heavy-handed royal badinage about the smallness of his person. The courtiers of the Winter Queen were accustomed to this sort of thing. Sir Thomas Roe submitted with a good grace to being called 'Honest fatt Thom,' and the Earl of Carlisle to 'thou ugly, filthy camel's face.' Certain of Sir Jacob Astley's clothes—the plain buff coat which he wore on his campaigns, and beneath it the leathern vest with sleeves enriched with heavy metallic braid — are still in the keeping of his descendants. It is evident from these garments that he was indeed an exceptionally small man.

When the political skies in England began to grow overcast, Sir Jacob returned to the service of his own King. He was made Governor of Plymouth, and in addition did valuable work both in 1639 and 1640 in mustering and organising the forces of the King against the Scots. When in 1642 the Civil War began, he was one of the comparatively small number of officers on either side who had any experience of actual warfare. His private convictions made him a whole-hearted partisan of the King: just as the convictions of another professional soldier, Philip Skippon of Foulsham - whom he must have known both in the Netherlands and as a neighbour of his family in Norfolk - brought him with equal fervour to the support of the Parliament.

3

At this time the head of the Astley family, and the owner of Melton Constable, was Sir Jacob's great-nephew, Sir Isaac Astley. He was twice married, to Rachel Messenger of Hackford and Bridget Coke of Holkham, but had no children by either wife. His heir was his brother Edward, who was born in 1603, and in 1639 married Elizabeth, the only daughter of their great-uncle Sir Jacob.

She was fifteen years younger than her husband, and it is possible that she had seldom or never been in England before her marriage. Her mother, Agnes Impel, may never have fully learnt the English language: at any rate she preferred to correspond with her daughter in Dutch. And Elizabeth herself may have spoken with a marked Dutch accent. The spelling of the entries in her Bible, from which I have derived much information, was not worse than that of many gentlewomen of her day; but seventeenth-century spelling often tended to be phonetic, and several of her efforts — for instance 'shortsh' for church, and 'shield' for child — suggest that her ear was attuned to Dutch rather than to English inflexions of speech.

Edward Astley accompanied Sir Jacob on his first expedition to the north in 1639. His marriage to his young cousin in Holland had already been arranged; and in April of that year he wrote to her from York the earliest of his surviving letters.

Most deare Cossin,

Be pleased to accept of these few lines from him that doth most intirely love and honour you; and could you butt see the fountain from whence they issue and are derived, you should finde farr mor than this scribbled paper is any way able to expresse, or my meane and weake abilities can utter. Onely thus much I will be bould to aver, there is none breathing whome I more desire to see and injoy than your most desired self, or to speake truer none but your self.

Sweet Cossin, if God and the windes will permitt I resolve ere long to kisse your hands at Skedam, and be your servant to attend you into England. In the meane time deare Cossin be pleased to retaine him in your good opinnion who is and will be until death

Your most affectionate Cossin
and faithfull Servant

Yorke 22th of   Edw. Astley.
Aprill 1639

4

They were married in the little church at Melton Constable on the 27th of August by their uncle the Rev. Richard Astley, who held the family livings of Melton and Burgh. On the 7th of July 1640 their first son was born, and was christened Jacob after his grandfather, who stood sponsor together with Sir Isaac and the two grandmothers. It is unlikely that Sir Jacob attended the ceremony in person. Throughout that summer he was once more in the north, striving to train the troops whom he described as "all the arch-knaves of this Kingdom," the reluctant and disorderly levies who were to oppose the advancing Scots. Probably his son-in-law was again with him; but I can find no details of Edward Astley's activities until the 3rd of December 1641, when he was knighted by King Charles at Hampton Court. In the following month his elder brother Sir Isaac was created a baronet.

4

The prospect of any reconciliation between King and Parliament was now almost hopeless. And as the year 1642 advanced, it must have become clear, if it was not clear already, that in the approaching conflict the two younger Astleys and their distinguished great-uncle would fight on opposite sides. The whole climate of opinion in Norfolk was Puritan and Parliamentarian. Of the twelve members returned to the Long Parliament for the county of Norfolk and its five boroughs — Norwich, Great Yarmouth, King's Lynn, Thetford and Castle Rising — only two adhered to the royal cause. The Royalist gentry — the Pastons, the L'Estranges, the Spelmans, the few Catholic families — were a small minority, quickly rendered powerless. Their neigh-

MELTON CONSTABLE

The church in Melton Constable Park, from Ladbrooke's drawing c. 1820

bours, loyal in theory to the Crown, could not at this juncture support the King. His opponents in Norfolk included Hobart of Blickling, Wodehouse of Kimberley, Coke of Holkham, Palgrave of North Barningham, Walpole of Houghton, Holland of Quidenham, Windham of Felbrigg, Potts of Mannington, Gawdy of East Harling — the list might be lengthened indefinitely. All these men were moderate in outlook. They would have been appalled if they had known what lay ahead —the execution of the King, the Commonwealth years of arbitrary or experimental government. But in 1642 their deeply-held political and religious convictions ranged them on the side of the Parliament.

Sir Isaac and Sir Edward Astley were entirely of the same way of thinking. One speculates on the arguments, the expostulations, perhaps the rueful but not unkindly jokes that they may have exchanged with old Sir Jacob, as he prepared to follow the King's cause wherever it might lead him. Even though few people on either side anticipated a long or a desperate war, there must have been a great sense of cleavage in a hitherto united family when he joined the King in the north, and his daughter and her husband remained in rebellious Norfolk. As soon as the Parliamentarian organisation got under way, both Sir Isaac and Sir Edward played important parts in it. The names of one or both are to be found on all the various County Committees by which money was collected, troops were raised, the estates of Royalists sequestered, and the rule of the Parliament enforced. When the group of eastern counties known as the Eastern Association was formed during the winter, both were placed on the important Standing Committee which sat at Cambridge and directed its operations to such good effect.

Some weeks before the actual outbreak of the war, the

7

King appointed Sir Jacob Astley to be Major General of the Foot. He remained a mainstay of the royal armies to the very end—resolute, cool-headed, absolutely dependable; the greatest possible contrast, in fact, to some of his colleagues, those temperamental grandees, those courtiers and politicians who did such irreparable damage to the King's cause. No man was held in higher regard by his fellow officers, more loved by his own troops or more respected by his opponents. Clarendon has depicted him for all time. "Sir Jacob Astley was an honest, brave, plain man, and as fit for the Office he exercised, of Major General of the Foot, as Christendom yeilded; and was so generally esteemed; very discerning and prompt in giving Orders, as the occasions required, and most chearful, and present in any Action. In Council he used few, but very pertinent words; and was not at all pleased with the long Speeches usually made there; and which rather confounded, than inform'd his understanding: so that he rather collected the ends of the Debates, and what he was himself to do, than enlarged them by his own Discourses; though he forbore not to deliver his own mind."

The impression left by Clarendon's words is confirmed by the splendid portrait painted by Van Dyck in 1640, and still in the possession of Sir Jacob's descendants—the martial features and upright active body, the vigorous greying hair and moustache and beard, the subtle harmony of yellow and brown and the steely glint of armour. It is confirmed likewise by his words before Edgehill, the opening battle of the war: "O Lord, Thou knowest how busy I must be this day. If I forget Thee, do not Thou forget me. March on, boys."

The earlier months of 1643 proved an anxious time for the newly-formed Eastern Association. There were movements of disaffection within its borders, particularly at Lowesttoft and King's Lynn, against which Cromwell, who was already marked out as the leading spirit in the Association, took swift and decisive action. An army had to be assembled, equipped and trained from men who came forward readily enough to defend their own farms or weaving-looms, but were often far from willing to campaign in distant counties. During the summer the Royalist successes in Lincolnshire assumed alarming proportions, with the loss of Gainsborough and the southward advance of Newcastle's army. In August the town of King's Lynn declared for the King, and withstood a siege of several weeks before it capitulated.

Sir Edward Astley was not, like his father-in-law, a professional soldier. But he had gained some military experience against the Scots, and now played an active part in raising troops for the Association, and commanding his own company in the field. There have survived a few of the letters which he wrote at this time to his wife; and as they are entirely unpublished, and throw some interesting light on the progress of the war, I am printing them here in full. The earliest are addressed "For my most deare and lovinge wife the Lady Astley at Bale." It appears that she was living at this village in company with her husband's mother, to whom he invariably sent his humble duty. "My brother and sister," to whom messages were also sent, were Sir Isaac and his wife at Melton Constable. Dorothy was an unmarried sister who lived with them. "Poore ffranck" was his own small daughter, who was born in 1642 and died at the age of three.

They were to have five more children in the coming years, but none lived more than a few days.

The first letter was written from Downham Market on the 22nd of May. On the following day he was to march his company to Wisbech, on the confines of their own county, while other troops were to press forward to join Cromwell in Lincolnshire.

Deare Harte

Having the Oportunity of sendinge unto thee by a Neighbor of ours, goodman Olborough, who by Chance came unto me when I was att supper, I could not lett slip the Occasion without a line or two unto thee to lett thee know that (praysed be God) I am in good health att this Present and have received orders to march with my Colonells Company and my owne unto Wisbidge to morrow. I heare that the Companies of volunteres under his Regiment are to March unto Colonell Cromwell into Lincolnshire, butt the Trayned bandes which are three (my Colonells Company, my owne and Seriant Maiors) are to remaine att Wisbidge for the securinge of our County. I hope in God to see thee att Bale by the latter ende of this weke, till which time I bid thee most Hartily ffarwell, and will ever rest

thy intirely lovinge Husband

Downeham this   Edw. Asteley
22th of May, 1643

I prethe sweet Harte remember my Humble unto my Mother and my love unto our bratts.

The next letter was written from Whittlesea near Peterborough, and gives some idea of the indiscipline of the troops at this early stage of the war. It was the state of things against which Cromwell so strongly inveighed, and was often due to the failure of the county authorities to forward sufficient pay-money and supplies. The Lord General, to whom Astley was going to report, was the Earl of Manchester, lately appointed to command the forces of the Eastern Association.

Deare Hart

I am this morning ridinge post unto my Lord Generall, who we heare is att Northampton, to informe him of the condition of our Regiment, which is very ill att this present, the soldiers doinge what they list, havinge the power in theyre owne handes. Besides we have certaine intelligence of eleven Colours that came into Stamforde yesterday, which is within 9 miles of us, so as if we be drawne from this place they will quickly possese themselves thereof, and are soone likely to brake into Norfolk or any part of the Association. I shall know when I speake with my Lord Generall whether we shall goe from this place or no, and give thee spedy advertisement thereof; in the meane time with my intire affections unto thy self and our little ones with my Humble duty unto my Mother in great hast I rest

Dear Hart

thy intirely lovinge Husband

Witlesey this   Edw: Astley
17th of June

Three days later Astley was back at Wisbech. The Queen, who had landed in the north earlier in the year, was now on her way to Oxford with money, arms and troops to reinforce her husband. She had reached the Royalist stronghold of Newark, and there was a plan that all the available

Parliamentarian forces should join to intercept her. Nothing came of it. The commands of the various districts were hopelessly disunited; and the whole current of the war appeared to be running against the Parliament, with the death of John Hampden after Chalgrove Field, the defeat of the Fairfaxes at Adwalton Moor, the almost successful treachery of Sir John Hotham and his son at Hull. All these discouragements are reflected in the three letters which follow, together with Astley's profound desire that God might 'putt an ende to these our miseries.' He was echoing, in a less eloquent strain, the words of Sir William Waller's unforgettable letter to Sir Ralph Hopton, his old friend and present adversary: 'The great God, which is the searcher of my heart, knows with what a sad sense I go upon this service, and with what a perfect hatred I detest this war without an enemy.'

Dear Hart

We are to drawe up all our fforces in these partes by to morrow night unto Bourne in Lincolneshire, beinge some 24 miles from this place, there beinge more Trayned bands sent for to come up theather where we are to meet with Colonell Cromwell. What will be there concluded on as yett we know nott; but it is conceived all the fforces in this County, the Ile of Ely, Cambrigeshire and Huntinton are to joyne with the Nottingham Army to impeach the Quenes advance unto Oxforde, who is allready come as ffar as Newarcke. Sir Willm Waller hath lately given a great defeate unto Sir Ralph Hopton, and my Lorde of Essex is within 5 miles of the Kinges Army, so as there will some thinge be acted very suddenly. I pray God turns all thinges to the best.

Thus Deare Harte with my best affections unto thy self, my Humble duty unto my Mother, my kind love unto my Brother and Sister and all my ffriendes in generall, I rest

   thy most affectionate Loving Husband
Wisbidge this   Edw: Asteley
20th of June 1643

My Deare Sweet Harte

 I am this day preparinge to march away with 12 foot Companies to Rockingham and so to Lester to joyne with my Lord Grey and Colonell Cromwells forces, to stop the Quenes advance towards Oxforde whom we heare is as ffar as Beaver [Belvoir] Castle, so as itt is thought we shall not come soone enough thether butt the busines will be desided before our cominge. Ther is a great devision in hir Army, the ffrench and English can nott well agree together. I pray God turns all things to his glory and to the Kingdomes and our goods. Deare Harte time will not permit to wright any more unto thee, onely I conclude with my prayers to Allmigty God for his blessinge and protection of thee and ours and all that belonge unto us. I bid thee farwell and rest

    Deare Harte
   thy most intirely lovinge Husband
     till Death

       Edw: Asteley
Peterborough this first day of July 1643
I prethe deare Harte remember my humble duty unto my Mother, my kinde love unto my Brother and sister and Sister Dorothy and Uncle and Aunt

and all our ffriends in generall, not forgetting my best affections unto thy self and our two little ones. I imagine Jacob doth sometimes aske for his Dadd butt poore ffrancke can say nothinge. Sweet Hart thou shall heare from me as soone as I can. I prethe Cheare up thy self and I pray God send us a happy meetinge.

------◆------

My Deare Sweet Harte

We are now advanced againe to Peterborough and are ready to march to Rockingham, 14 miles from this place, and so to joyne with Sir Myles Hobart and the rest of our fforces att Lester; butt I feare we shall have much trouble to gett our men to march as farr as Ashby dolosouch [de la Zouch] and the Kinge hath sent Prince Rupert with 4000 horse and foot from Oxforde to meet hir and to conduct hir thether. The Earle of Essex we heare hath likewise sent the like number after him, and since that the Kinge hath sent more forces after the Earles, and the Earle againe hath sent as many after them, and is removed with the whole body of his Army betwene the Kings army and the way the quene is to come with hir forces unto him. What will be the issue God onely knoweth. My Lord ffayrfax hath had lately the worst of itt beinge forced for want of Ammunition to forsake Leeds and retreat to Hull. I presume you have heard of the apprehension of Sir John Hotham and his sonne and sendinge them up to the Parliament. They had a plott to betray Hull Lincolne and Nottingham to the Kings party, butt God by his allseinge providence prevented them. I besetch God in his due time to putt an end to these our miseries, and send us again if itt be his blessed will a happy meetinge. More I have not sweet Harte att this present, butt the remembrances of my best wishes and affections unto thy self and our little ones, my humble duty unto my Mother, and my kinde love unto all our ffriends in generall I rest ever

Deare Harte
thy most intirely lovinge Husband
till death

Edw: Asteley

Peterborough the 8 of July 1643

I thanke little Jacob for his penny he sent me. I pray God in heaven to blesse him and all of us.

The Royalist pressure was steadily increasing. Peterborough was threatened, and a considerable force had occupied Burghley House, the Earl of Exeter's great mansion on the outskirts of Stamford. At this point Cromwell counter-attacked, and captured Burghley House on July 24th. I have not previously come across any contemporary description of this episode, of which Astley gives an unusually detailed account in his next letter.

My Deare Sweet Hart

Our Regiment marched on Sunday last from Peterborough to Burly Howse within a mile of Stamforde, where were gotten together about 400 of the Caveleirs. We summoned them by a trumpett on Sunday morning by breake of Day to deliver up the place, and we would give them quarter, which if they refused, if the Ordinance were once bent uppon them they were to expect no mercy butt to be putt all unto the sworde. They answered us againe that they would fight itt out unto the last man before they would yeld up the place. As soone as day appeared we began to play uppon them with our Ordinance, and gave them I beleve above a hundred shott; butt I beleve itt did no great execution by reason of the vastnes of the Howse, for they still showted upon every shott that was made upon them. About 12 a Clocke we aproched uppon them in 3 severall places, and our men assalted them with such Corage that by 3 a Clocke in the afternoone they sownded a parley, and after some consultation our trumpett answered them with the like; butt such was the madness of our soldiers for pillage that they brake in uppon them and fell a plunderinge. We took 3 hundred prissoners whereof 40 were officers, the Commander in Chefe Colonell Welby, and a knight whose name I have forgotten. We lost not above 4 men, butt we have som 20 or 30 sore wounded, and we cannot heare of many killed of theirs. This is the substance in short of this action. We are att this present at Stamford, and we expect to returne againe shortly to Peterborough, and I hope then to se thee att Bale. I bought this horse of a soldier which will serve thy Coach if he had a little more flesh of his back. I prethe sweet hart send my man unto me as soone as thou canst. Thus with remembrance of my best affections unto thy self and our little ones, my humble duty unto my Mother, and my kind love unto the rest of our ffriends I rest

Deare Hart

thy intirely lovinge Husband

till Death

Stamford this

29 of July

Edw: Asteley

At this point the letters break off, and there are no more until the summer of 1645. It is useless to speculate upon Sir Edward's activities during the interval — whether his company formed part of the force which presently besieged King's Lynn: to what extent he was involved in the later stages of the war, as it shifted to and fro across the kingdom: whether he and his father-in-law were at any time opposed in battle. The remaining letters, three in number, were written when the war was at last drawing to its close, just at the time of the decisive battle of Naseby. It would seem that Sir Edward was now commanding a reserve force, subject to the orders of the local Committees both at Cambridge and Norwich.[1] He had received orders to advance to Spalding, and arrived there on June 13th. On that same day the battle of Naseby was fought, and proved disastrous in every way to the King's fortunes.

By this time Lady Astley had moved from Bale to another house belonging to the family at Hindolvestone. There is pathos in her husband's anxiety about the health of their little daughter 'ffranck,' who died two days after the last letter was written.

Sweet Hart

I received an Order last night from the Committee att Cambridge for the Advance of my regiment to Spaldinge. I have wrott unto the Committee att Norwich, which if I have theire aprobation and consent therunto, then I must uppon Monday next march thether. I thinke there will be no danger in

1. The Committee at Cambridge reported to Parliament on June that "we had formerly sent to the Counties to raise their Horse and Dragoons to their borders as nigh Cambridge as may be." Rushworth's Collections. vi. 38.

goinge thether, the Kings Army beinge retreated back againe as farr as Northampton, and Sir Thomas ffairfax is advanced with his Army, beinge 7000 Horsse and dragoons and 8000 foott, very neare unto Northampton too. I prethe sweet Hart sende Will or John Woolno unto me, and sende by him my Dressinge which Armiger brought from London last, and allso one shirt moer. Lett him ride on my great geldinge, and if itt be possible to be here early on Monday next. Thus with my best affections unto thee

I rest

thy ever lovinge Husband

Wisbidge 7th June   Edw: Asteley
1645

We heare the Scotch army is allso come to Nottingham.

———————◆———————

Sweet Harte

I have received Orders from our Committee to advance with my Regiment to Spalldinge, and Colonell Willton have received like orders to advance with his Regiment unto Whittlesea. To morrow we shall be uppon our March; as for the Kings Army they are so far distant that for these two dayes we have nott hearde of them, and itt is verily thought that by this time there hath bene some ingadgement betwene Sir Thomas ffairfax and the Kinge. I prethe Deare Harte trowble nott thy self for any danger, for by the Grace of God I shall be as safe att Spalldinge as if I were at Hillderston. I beleve we shall all retreat within this weeke att furthest; and whensoever I have any opportunitty to write thou shalt heare from me. In the meane time with my best affections unto thy self, my duty unto my Mother and love unto Jacob and little ffranke, I shold be glad to heare of hir recovery,

I rest

thy ever lovinge Husband

Wisbidge ye   Edw: Asteley
9th of June 1645

My Deare Sweet Hart

Last night I came to Spallding, and havinge the opportunity to write by Lawrance Bonde, I could nott choose butt sende 2 or 3 lynes unto thee. For newes itt is thus: the Kinge with his Army lyss att Baintry, within 5 miles of Hillmorton; he takes the Advantage of the Hills and will not fight untill he hath more forces come unto him, which he hath sent for out of all the Garrisons ther aboutes. Sir Thomas ffairfax lyes with his Army about Stony Strattforde, very neere unto the Kinge who likewise followinge his Example hath sent for all the Yorkeshire Horsse, Sir Willm Bruertons, Nottingham, Darby and Lincolnshire Horsse; so that he hath by this time a gallant Army. Itt is dayly expected to heare of the Armyss ingadgements. We ly here very secure from danger, havinge no Enemy neare us, and expect very shortly to be called home againe. I prethe sweet Harte trowble not thy self, for by the Grace of God I make no question butt to see thee very shortly. In the meane time with my best affections unto thy self, my dutty unto my Mother, and my kinde love unto Jacob and ffranck I rest

thy ever lovinge Husbande

Spaldinge June 14 1645   Edw: Asteley

Sir Jacob Astley.

Published Aug. 1801 from a Plate by Worlidge by T.& H. Rodd. 17. Little Newport St. Leicester St.   Proof.

SIR JACOB later LORD ASTLEY
engraved by Worlidge from the painting by Van Dyck

During these years Sir Jacob Astley had ever been in the forefront of the war. As the reward of his services he was raised to the peerage, on the 4th of November 1644, as Baron Astley of Reading, the town which he had captured and garrisoned in the previous year. The Letters Patent, still in the possession of his family, splendidly engrossed and bearing the Great Seal, give no indication that they were drawn up at Oxford at a time when the King could command only a fragment of his realm. They recite in detail Sir Jacob's exploits under various foreign powers, and in more recent years his fidelity to his own sovereign and his good service against the machinations of wicked rebels. All his actions are given — Edgehill (which is called Kineton), Brentford, Newbury, the bridges of Gosworth and Cropredy, 'præclara illa et insanguis prope Lestithiel in comitatu nostro Cornubia victoria,' and all the rest. And it speaks also of his son, Sir Bernard, who had so distinguished himself at the siege of Bristol — 're vera tali patre dignus.'

The next year brought misfortune to Lord Astley as well as to the cause he served. At Naseby, where he commanded the main body of infantry in the centre, his skill and courage could not avert a calamitous defeat. Later in the year his son Sir Bernard met his death at the second siege of Bristol, when the city was recaptured by Fairfax. An entry in the Bible of his sister Elizabeth briefly tells the tale. 'My brother Ser barnard Astley was tækon prisner att the seidsh of bristowe by the parlement and was caried att the bath wheare hee dyed of 10 wounds and was beried theare. he died the 16 of September 1645.' Their mother, the old Dutch lady Agnes Impel, was also in the besieged city. She was enabled to leave, and made her way to the security of her daughter's house in distant Norfolk. 'My mother the lady Astley came to hildelveston owt of the Towne of bristowe when itt was besieged by the parlement and was tækon by them in a fewe days after.'

Still Lord Astley fought on, trying to rally the remnants of the King's supporters in the west and along the Welsh borders. At last, on the 21st of March, 1646, he was defeated and taken prisoner at Stow on the Wold by a Parliamentarian force under Sir Thomas Brereton and Colonel Morgan. Apart from the reduction of a few isolated garrisons, it was the last action of the war. Afterwards the old hero, seated on a drum, uttered words which the victorious group around him may well have recalled in years to come. 'You have done your work, boys; you may go play, unless you fall out among yourselves.'

He was imprisoned for a time at Warwick Castle. Liked and respected as he was by his adversaries, one cannot suppose that his confinement was very rigorous. While he was at Warwick the King rode in disguise out of beleaguered Oxford, and after some days of wandering gave himself up to the Scots army. In June came the capitulation of Oxford. When Sir Thomas Glemham, the Governor of the city, was discussing the terms of surrender with Fairfax, he was able to arrange for Lord Astley to be covered by the articles as if he had been amongst the garrison. These articles provided that the defenders of Oxford might pass unmolested, with their arms and equipage, 'to their Houses or Friends, without any prejudice to their Friends for receiving them.' Reasonable terms were also laid down by which they could compound for their estates and withdraw them from sequestration.

A letter from Sir Edward Astley about this transaction has survived. Apparently he had gone to Warwick to see his father-in-law, and if possible to hasten his release. On the 6th of July he wrote thus to his wife:

Deare Harte

ffor my Jorny to London itt is now otherwise determined of, the Generall Sir Thomas ffayrefax havinge promised Sir Thomas Glemham uppon the surrender of Oxforde to procure my Lorde to be comprehended within those articles, and my lorde hath wrott unto Sir Thomas ffayrefax concerninge the same, butt hath nott as yett received his answer. My lorde hath desired me, in case he receives itt nott by to morrow, that the day followinge beinge Tusday I should goe unto Oxforde, which is about 30 miles from this place, to solicite my lordes busines with the Generall there; so as itt will be the latter ende of the next weeke before I shall see thee att Hillderston which is the earnest desire of

Sweet Harte

thy affectionate lovinge Husbande

Warwick July 6 1646   Edw: Asteley

I prethe sweet harte present humble servis unto my lady, my duty to my Mother and my love unto little Jacob and his sweet harte.

Whether or not Sir Edward had to go to Oxford to interview Fairfax, the undertakings given at the surrender of Oxford were duly carried out; and we read in his wife's Bible that 'my father the lord Astley came from warwik cassell to hildelveston the 18 day of july 1646.'

7

They all settled down happily enough at Hindolvestone—

the old Cavalier and his wife, their daughter and her Parliamentarian husband, and little Jacob their grandson. The war was over; the political differences between the two men seem never to have diminished their personal affection; and family life was resumed as though it had never been interrupted.

The business of Lord Astley's composition for his property in Kent became an important preoccupation, and dragged on for a long while. Like his daughter, he was in the habit of recording events in his Bible, a much-worn volume with a vignette upon the title-page of an army on the march. It was not until almost two years after his surrender that he was able to write: 'I mad my Composition with Mr. Stevenes upon Tusday the 8th of ffebruary 1648 about 2 in the afternoone.' A letter in the Bodleian Library, written on April 28th to his Parliamentarian neighbour Sir John Potts of Mannington, seems to confirm this: 'As to London, I and my businesses there, I well hope, hath bidden it farewell for a long time. Concerning £400 that I owe in London against August next, I have already taken order for the payment of it, and shall not make use of any moneys out of Holland, being my wife's, which I am very loath to diminish.' His estate had been valued at £200 a year, and under the articles of Oxford he was obliged to pay a capital sum of two years' value.

Shortly after this the second Civil War broke out, with risings in Kent and Essex, and some stirrings of discontent in Norfolk. But Lord Astley had given his parole, and made no move. He remained quietly at Hindolvestone until the summer of 1650, when he and his wife went to live at their house in Maidstone. This was known as the Palace, a former monastic property which had been given to an earlier Astley by Queen Elizabeth. I do not know when or in what circumstances it was inherited by Lord Astley.

During those four years in Norfolk he had grown deeply attached to his grandson. Little Jacob was then his only descendant in the second generation, the child in whom all his hopes were centred. He wrote to him often from Maidstone, and a few letters and a poem have chanced to survive. They show the sweet nature and simplicity of heart which this veteran soldier had preserved through all the vicissitudes of his life. These letters, like those of Sir Edward Astley, are wholly unpublished, and I am printing them in full.

The earliest is the poem, dated from Maidstone on the 16th of October 1650.

My derest Grandchild, all that I shall looke
Or expect from thee, is to learne thy booke,
The only way to make thee knowe
The hight of thinges, and slite the lowe;
Which being attaind the endes are thyne,
Only the Comfort shalbe myne.
And in the Springe of the next yeere
Thy parents promies to be heere,
Whear appeles, peares and plumes are plenty,
And no rare frutes are here termed dainty;
Duringe which time no Scoole shall fright thee,
But we will strive how to delight thee.
The Towne is stronge, and all thinges fitting,
Almost in as good state as Weetinge. 1
Here's a grene meadowe for your Nage,
Fencht for to keep the wildest Stagge:
In breefe, my Jacob, the great want that I
Sustaine is thy good Companie.
And so, my Boy, once more Adewe
Till thow meet me or I meet you;

1. Weeting was (and is) a small and remote village in Norfolk.

25

And thus my prittie, little frende,
I expect your answer, at some two yeres end,
Who is thy
Owlde lovinge Grandfather
Jacob Astley.

The next letter, although only dated 'from Maidston, the day after Saint Davids daye,' clearly belongs to 1651.

for Littell Sir Jacob Asteley, Knight of the Wheel of Forteune.

I am advertised, by certain of my Skoutes, sent forth to discover these Costes, that you intend to invad and enter upon these Terrietories.

Know thearfor, that I do not forbid you, but if you dar to be so venterus,

By these, I challendge you, to meet me upon Boxly Hilles, 3 myles from this place, which ar near as high as Edge Hille, whear under thear was once fought a Battell; thear you shall finde me compleatly armed with Horse, Launce and a paier of Pistoles, Sword and Pollaxe, and uppon my Crest a Towne Toppe - and bringe you a London Boye with you, and I will bring a Maydeston Boye with me, for both our seaconds; my Quarrell to you shallbe in the Honour and Deffence of the ffaier Maides of this Towne; appoynt you the time for metinge, and so I remayne until I see you

Your faier Adversary
Owld Jacob Asteley

I pray comend me to your trusty Servants Tom Woods, Hary Claiburne and all your football plaiers.

The plans for young Jacob's visit in the spring, however, met with a disagreeable interruption. The country was still restless and discontented, the young King active in Scotland, and many Royalists hoping for his invasion of England — which in fact occurred in the summer, only to end in utter defeat at Worcester. Order was given that certain 'old Cavaliers' in Kent should be taken into custody, and secured 'in one of your garrisons furthest from their houses, and from the places where they have any influence.' Despite the parole he had given in 1646, and his honourable observance of it ever since, Sir Jacob Astley — the Parliament would not of course acknowledge the peerage bestowed upon him by the dead King — was included in the order. He recorded in his Bible that 'I was brought a prisener to Ledys Castell the 26 of April beinge a Saterday 1651.' From thence he was taken to London and confined in the Fleet Prison, but released at the end of May and allowed to go home to Maidstone, on giving bail in the sum of £1,000 with two sureties of £500 apiece.

His daughter visited him after his return, and one hopes that she brought Jacob with her. She was back in Norfolk by the end of July, and had written to tell him that they proposed to send Jacob to the Grammar School at Norwich. He replied on the 30th of July:

My der, and ondly Daughter,
    I am very glad, as also your mother, to hear that you had so good a Journe homewards. I have wrott to your husband, that will tell you all your Acquaintance here ar very well, unto whom I have delivered your Salutes to them all. I mutch wonder, that you durst ventuer to send Jacob so far from you to Skoole as Norwidge. Full littell thincke you how

his bumbe will suffer, for they ar all churlish masters thear and will whipe boyes without mercie. I hope he will remember my meadison to lay a cowld ston to a warme bume, which will take a way all smartinge. Two daies past I had a letter from your brother Isaack, my daughter thear is with childe... Now my der daughter, not having further to wright of, your mother salutes you. All your frendes here often remembers you. I praie remember me kindly to Besse Bacon, and all your servants, and all my frendes in generall. And God Almightie preserve you. And I rest

My ondly daughter
Your very lovinge father
Jacob Asteley

His only surviving son Isaac, mentioned in the foregoing letter, had recently married Anna, the daughter of a Surrey knight named Sir Francis Stydolfe. Their child, yet another Jacob, was born in January 1652, and is referred to in the next letter. It is a little note, jokingly addressed to 'my derly loving granson Jacob Asteley Esquier Cheffe Scoller at Norwidge': and the boy's mother has endorsed upon it that it was the last letter he ever received from his grandfather.

My der littell Jacob I must thanck you very kindly for your letter, and did not a littell wonder, that in so short a time you could have wrott so well. And in your praies I must say that if England could broock a Kinge you mought be his Secretary. I must tell you that I have now an other littell Jacob but he is but a Baby, and will be long before he proves a London Boy, or be fitt for Campinge (1), neyther

1. Camping was the early Norfolk variety of football which continued to be played well into the nineteenth century.

28

shall he growe more in my affection than your Selfe
is, which is assured by

Your very lovinge Grandfather

Jacob Asteley

Gett lerninge, then non can deseeve thee
And thou shalt keepe what others leeve thee.

London

this first of february 1652.

Less than a month afterwards, as is recorded in his
daughter's Bible, 'my deare father dyed att Maidston of a
viollent fitt of the stone the 27 day of febrewary 1652.' He
was buried in Maidstone Church, where there is an im-
pressive monument to his memory.

There remains one more letter in the series, written to
Jacob jointly by his parents in 1652 or 1653.

Sonne Jacob

We received your letter and take itt kindly from
you that you write so often unto us; your Horse
shalbe well looked unto and a Drum shall be bought
for you if Hempton ffayre will afforde one; butt the
worst is I am afraide when you come home at
Christmas you will ffollow the Drum so much that
you will drum out all the learning that you will
bringe from Norwich with you, so that I feare itt
will cost you more scoole butter then the Drum is
worth to beate itt into your head againe when you
returne to Norwich. We hope you will follow your
booke apace that you may be able to make an eloquent Spech before the Ruffs (1) the next yeare: you

1. I think 'the Ruffs' may have been a term for the Mayor and Alder-
men of Norwich. At the Guild Day each year it was customary for
one of the boys at the Grammar School to deliver a speech of con-
gratulation to the newly elected Mayor.

must remember us very kindly unto my Cossin
Stewarte and his wife, and so we pray God to blesse
you and bid you ffarwell; your Lovinge ffather and
mother

      Elisabeth Asteley   Edw: Asteley

we have each of us sent you sixpence a peece to
buye you Cake withall

Soon Jacob was the only survivor of the three generations
around whom this study has been written. On the 15th of
March 1654 his father died, suddenly and unexpectedly at
the age of fifty-one, in the course of his year as High Sheriff
of Norfolk. The boy at Norwich School was left alone to
carry on the family; and on the death of his childless uncle
Sir Isaac in 1659 he succeeded to Melton Constable and all
the Norfolk estates. In 1657 he went to Cambridge; at the
'Restoration he was created a baronet; he built the present
house at Melton Constable, represented the county of Norfolk in a long series of Parliaments, and continued to flourish
until his ninetieth year. Far into the eighteenth century,
when the second of the Georges was on the throne, he must
have retained vivid memories of his kind old grandfather,
who had been born before the coming of the Armada, and
had seen Queen Elizabeth, and sustained so gallantly the
failing fortunes of King Charles.

Notes

---◆---

The late Mr Ketton Cremer's footnotes have been printed with the the text. The following notes have been added by the present editor.

p. 2 'They had two sons ...'

A third son, Thomas, is said to have died in Holland. Lord Hastings, '*Astley of Melton Constable 1236-1936*', mentions another son, also killed in the Netherlands, and a fifth who died in 1670.

p. 3 'Great nephew ...'

No evidence has been found that Edward was the great-nephew rather than the nephew of Sir Jacob. The Melton Constable register entries begin with Thomas, 'the sonne of Mr Isaac Asteley', baptised 12 October 1567, and include Jacob, baptised 28 March 1579, and Richard, baptised 20 February 1590/1. The marriage of Thomas Astley and Frances Deane took place on 18 June 1593; their first son, Francis, was baptised 26 January 1594/5, two daughters, Marie and Dorothie, followed in 1596 and 1597/8, and Isaac, the second son, was baptised on 3 August 1600. Thomas Astley, the son of Thomas Astley Esq., was buried on 12 April 1616, but his baptismal date is not recorded. Assuming that he was conceived in wedlock he could not have been born before the middle of May 1594. The baptism of Edward is likewise not recorded in the register, but according to his monument in Melton church he was the third son of Thomas Astley and died on 15 March 1653/4, which means that he was born between 16 March 1603/4 and 15 March 1604/5. There seems to be simply no room to make Francis, Isaac, and Edward Astley the great-nephews of Sir Jacob, and as

31

Mr Ketton-Cremer accepts that Isaac and Edward were brothers the most likely solution is that he made a rare and uncharacteristic slip, which he implicitly corrected later: R. W. Ketton-Cremer, 'Norfolk in the Civil War' p. 46.

p. 9   'Bale.'

The only house of any size recorded in the Hearth Tax assessment for 1664 was that occupied by George Bullen, gent., which had 8 hearths.

p. 14   'Sir Myles Hobart...'

Sir Miles was the brother of Sir John Hobart of Blickling and according to Ketton-Cremer (op. cit.) he inherited the family property at Intwood. In the index to 'Suffolk and the Great Rebellion' by Alan Everitt he is described as 'of Plumstead'.

p. 17   'Hindolvestone.'

The manor house of Hindolveston belonged to the priory of Norwich in the middle ages, and passed at the Dissolution to the Dean and Chapter who leased out the manor. This must be the house assessed at 16 hearths in the Hearth Tax of 1664 and occupied by Lady Elizabeth Astley, widow of Sir Edward. A map of 1704 (NRO, DC 11917) shows a 2½-storey porched house with an axial stack opposite the porch and another stack at the south end of the eastern side. Just to the north stands another 2½-storey range with central door and axial and south gable stacks. Neither of these buildings is easy to reconcile with the present building, which has short cross-wings at its ends, the northern one with shaped gables and a big attached stack on its north side, the southern much rebuilt, with stepped gables (the copings are probably modern), two modern stacks on the south wall, and a datestone of 1722. Most of the brickwork and details of the building suggest a date of about 1600. The great barn of the 1704 map seems to have been still there in 1887 but had gone by the early years of this century.

p. 24 'I do not know when...'

The property in Kent was that granted to John Astley (d. 1595) by Queen Elizabeth. His son Sir John was a member of the court of Queen Elizabeth of Bohemia, James I's daughter, whom Sir Jacob also served. The property came to Sir Jacob when Sir John died childless in 1639.

p. 25 'Weeting...'

Faden's map of 1797 shows both Weeting Castle and the church in ruins and it seems probable that the castle at least was already dilapidated in Sir Jacob's time. This may therefore be a rueful reference to the general decay of his estate at Maidstone.

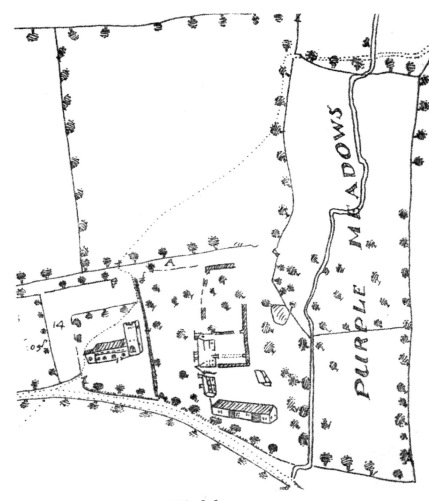

Hindolveston 1704

A portion of a map of Hindolveston made in 1704 and now in the Norfolk Record Office. It shows the old church (now ruined) and the manor-house to the west. (Some of the ink on the house has disappeared.) The manor-house was used by the Astleys during the Civil War and was the home of Elizabeth Astley after Sir Edward's death in 1654.

After the Restoration

At the Restoration in 1660 the young Jacob Astley found himself in possession of tolerably large estates, a brand-new baronetcy, and an old house. The fragmentary remains of the old building date from the early 16th century, but the Knyff-Kipp view of just before 1707 shows a single-range, seven-bay house with dormer windows, pedimented main windows, and shaped gables surmounted by a large finial, all suggesting a house of the late Elizabethan or the Jacobean period, say 1580-1620. These details, which are repeated in a slightly later print of the 18th century, may well represent a cosmetic updating of an older house. The clock-tower was added c. 1700. Knyff also shows a detached octagonal tower, to the south of the old range, which is perhaps a remnant of an early-16th-century house, and behind the old house and to the north are two courtyards with three $1\frac{1}{2}$-storey buildings with shaped or stepped gables, a barn, and a granary and dovehouse. On the extreme right of Knyff's engraving is the bath-house, a building in the Elizabethan style but gothicised later in the 18th century, and to the north of this the three rectangular stepped ponds with sluices may represent the formalised remnants of medieval fish-ponds. The moated site of the medieval manor-house, abandoned perhaps c. 1500 when the 'old' house was begun, is some 300 yards to the south-east and does not appear on Knyff. If the old house on the engraving represents the bulk of the house that young Jacob Astley inherited it was a manor-house of modest size. The late Lord Hastings, in his short history of the family, stated that 'finding the family home in ruins he [Sir Jacob] pulled down the greater part of it and started to build a new house, retaining one side of the old courtyarded house as servants' quarters and offices'. (1) The story that the house was sacked by 'parliamentary troops', repeated by Hussey in his *Country Life* article, may have sprung from a mistaken family conviction that the Melton Constable Astleys were royalists. It is extremely unlikely that the house of Sir Isaac, active for the parliamentary cause in Norfolk for the whole of the Civil War period, would have suffered depredations from the forces of his own side. It is more likely that the comparatively small size and old-fashioned nature of his old house convinced the young Sir Jacob that a completely new house was necessary. In the Hearth Tax returns of 1664 and 1666 the house is down as having only 11 hearths which means that there were at least 175 houses in the county, excluding large towns, with a greater number of hearths. It was smaller, for instance, than the neighbouring Thursford Hall (20 hearths), Wood Dalling Hall (17), Gunthorpe (17), Hindolveston, the home of his mother Lady Elizabeth Astley (16), and Burgh Parva Hall (14). (2) It was vastly inferior in size to the home of his wife Blanch Wodehouse, Kimberley Hall. (3) The Knyff engraving shows only two ranges of chimney-stacks, but it is likely that a house of the early 16th century, partly modernised c. 1600, would have considerably fewer hearths than a brand-new house of the period 1580-1640, which is when all those cited above were built. Moreover, according to Lord Hastings, Sir Jacob had begun to dismantle the old house in 1664; if this is correct, the 11 hearths would represent only that part of the old house still standing when the Hearth Tax assessment was made.

The new house was probably begun in the later 1660s. The architect is not known, although Hugh May, Christopher Wren, and Roger Pratt are possibilities; but it was also possible that Jacob was his own architect, using the professional services of master masons like the Edge dynasty, who had worked with Sir Roger Townshend at Raynham and were employed by his successor and by the Walpoles at Houghton in the post-Restoration period. The plaster ceiling in the Red Drawing Room is dated 1687, and may be the work of Edward Goudge, who probably worked at Felbrigg in 1687, Belton House, Lincolnshire in 1688, and Hintlesham Hall, Suffolk, c. 1690. The completion of the house, therefore, was shortly after 1687. According to Knyff's engraving, the principal garden to the south of the new house was both simpler and more axial in design than that of most great houses of the time; it was probably laid out in the 1670s and 1680s, and the simplicity may spring from the fact that it related to a new house on a new site. Working from Knyff's drawing one can estimate that the deer-proof wall enclosed about $3\frac{1}{2}$ acres; the central canal was about 23 yards wide and 130 yards long and lay between clipped evergreens, with a parterre of simple geometrical beds enhanced by statues and more clipped greens. A smaller formal garden containing four geometrical and two linear beds lay to the west of the house and was also walled, while the north entrance court contained a circular drive, probably of gravel, with a grass lawn. The canal was probably replenished from the three stepped ponds by means of sluices and underground pipes. Another circular drive stood at the east front of the house, and beyond it, and relating to the old house, was a walled kitchen garden.

In the 18th century, possibly after the death of Sir Jacob (1729) or more likely after that of his son Sir Philip (1739), the formal layout was dismantled and the park landscaped. An engraving, undated but probably after 1730 and certainly before 1757, (4) shows the house surrounded at a distance of

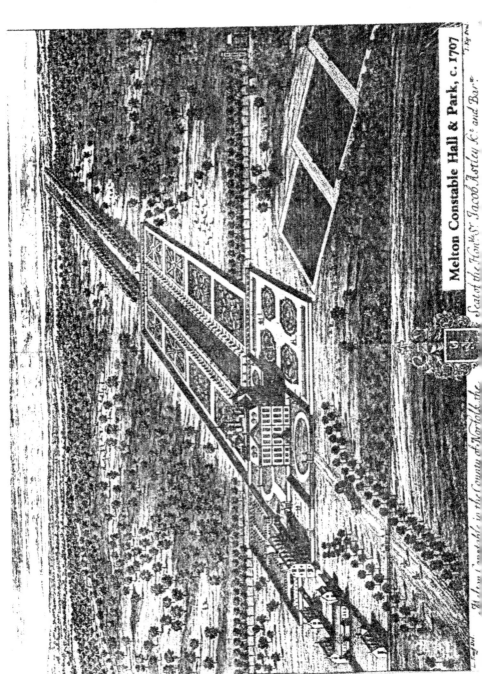

Melton Constable Hall & Park, c. 1707

Melton Constable in the County of Norfolk, the Seat of the Hon.ble S.r Jacob Astley K.t and Bar.t

Enlargement of the area depicting the old and new houses

30-40 feet by a wide, deep ha-ha that follows the shape of the building; walls, parterres, and canal have vanished. This considerably precedes the landscaping scheme provided by Capability Brown in 1764 (5), which cost Sir Edward Astley £2,500 and took five years to complete. The central lantern and cupola shown on both engravings and also on the model of the house now in the Rural Life Museum, Gressenhall, was dismantled at some time in the 18th century, perhaps during the alterations in the 1750s and 1760s which included erecting the west portico, remodelling the south entrance, and updating the interior. Extensions were built on the east side of the house in the early 19th century, and the gardens were terraced, balustraded, and laid out in the contemporary fashion in the 1840s.

Sir Jacob, besides building a new house, reorganised his farms, built houses and cottages, and consolidated his estates. In 1708 he sold his property in Kent which he had inherited when the last Lord Astley died in 1688. His grandson, Sir Jacob (1692-1760), was a man of letters, a musician (he played the cello), a patron of the arts, and a planter of trees. The marriage of his son Sir Edward (1729-1802) to Rhoda Delaval, though tragically short — she died aged 27 — eventually brought the Seaton Delaval estate in Northumberland to the family after the death of the last Lord Delaval in 1808. The marriage of Sir Jacob himself to Lucy Le Strange, co-heir of her brother Sir Henry Le Strange, was responsible for the barony of Hastings coming to the Astley family. With the death in 1542 of the 15th Lord Hastings the right to the barony fell into abeyance between his two sisters. The younger sister married Hamon Le Strange of Hunstanton, and the right descended through the Le Strange family. The direct male line ended with the death of Sir Henry Le Strange in 1760. In 1841 the House of Lords reported that the coheirs to the title were Henry L'Estrange, Styleman Le Strange and Sir Jacob Astley. The latter, the 6th baronet and known as 'the pocket Adonis', had the abeyance terminated in his favour and became the 16th baron Hastings. According to his great-grandson 'An autocratic disposition combined with a certain intolerance of persons not so energetic as himself got him into difficulties at times'. Immediately after his death his son Jacob (1822-71) married a gold-digger from Brighton who 'caused fearful dissension in the family'. A series of premature deaths led to the grandson of the 16th Lord Hastings succeeding to the title as the 20th baron within 16 years of his grandfather's death. George Manners Astley (1857-1904) established the stud at Melton and won the 1885 Derby with the horse called Melton; he was a fine shot, and was one of the first Norfolk owners of a motor-car. He also restored the parish church, turned the gallery connecting the old house and the new house into a kitchen wing and added a block at the east end of the gallery. The 21st Lord Hastings added two further small extensions to make the east wing of the house a self-contained dwelling. He sold the house to the Duke of Westminster in 1950; the present owner, Roger Gawn, is converting the east wing into private dwellings and beginning the long process of restoration of Sir Jacob Astley's magnificent house.

Notes

1. Lord Hastings, '*Astley of Melton Constable*'; C. Hussey, *Country Life* 64, 1928, 368-9

2. F. Blomefield, *History of Norfolk* ix, says that Elizabeth married Henry Clifton of Toftrees, and this is followed in G. H. Dashwood, '*The Visitation of Norfolk....1563*', i, 297. Clifton was a widower with three daughters and a son of unsound mind; he died in 1670, and there is no mention of Elizabeth in his will dated 1668, neither is she described as his widow on her monument in Melton Constable church.

3. This is the Tudor Kimberley, not the present house. An inventory of 1588 gives hall, great parlour, chapel, armoury, and 17 bedchambers, besides unmentioned service rooms.

4. On this engraving the west front has an open set of stairs leading up to the Grand Storey, instead of the portico built in 1757. If this is the print to which Hussey refers (*Country Life* 64, 1928, 370) it can hardly be of c. 1720, unless Sir Jacob were a very advanced gardener or the printmaker extremely prophetic.

5. Dorothy Stroud, '*Capability Brown*' (1984), 112.

The Melton Constable area on Faden's Map of 1797